How Art

Pa[...]d

www.heinemann.co.uk

Visit our website to find out more information about Heinemann Library books.

To order:

☎ Phone 44 (0) 1865 888066

🖹 Send a fax to 44 (0) 1865 314091

💻 Visit the Heinemann Bookshop at www.heinemann.co.uk to browse our catalogue and order online.

First published in Great Britain by Heinemann Library, Halley Court, Jordan Hill, Oxford OX2 8EJ, a division of Reed Educational and Professional Publishing Ltd.
Heinemann is a registered trademark of Reed Educational & Professional Publishing Ltd.

OXFORD MELBOURNE AUCKLAND JOHANNESBURG BLANTYRE
GABORONE IBADAN PORTSMOUTH (NH) USA CHICAGO

Designed by Celia Floyd
Illustrations by Jo Brooker/Ann Miller
Originated by Ambassador Litho Ltd.
Printed and bound in Hong Kong/China

06 05 04 03 02   06 05 04
10 9 8 7 6 5 4 3 2 1   10 9 8 7 6 5 4 3 2
ISBN 0 431 11522 2 (hardback)   ISBN 0 431 11528 1 (paperback)

British Library Cataloguing in Publication Data

Flux, Paul
   How artists use pattern and texture.
   1.Repetitive patterns (Decorative arts) in art – Juvenile literature 2.Repetitive patterns (Decorative arts)
   Juvenile literature
   I.Title
   745.4

Acknowledgements

The Publishers would like to thank the following for permission to reproduce photographs:
AKG, London: pp16, 24; Boomalli Aboriginal Artists. Purchased with the assistance of funds from National Gallery admission charges and commissioned in 1987. Collection: National Gallery of Australia, Canberra: p12; Bridgeman Art Library: Alan Bowness Hepworth Estate/Bristol City Museum and Art Gallery p18, Arts Council Collection, Hayward Gallery, London/Bridget Riley p21, British Library, London p27, Christie's Images Collection/ARS, NY and DACS, London 2001 p9, Scottish National Gallery of Modern Art, Edinburgh/© ADAGP, Paris and DACS, London 2001 p19, State Russian Museum, St. Petersburg p13; Corbis: bottom left p7, Bojan Brecelj p5, © ADAGP, Paris and DACS, London 2001 p20, Angelo Hornak p11, Matthew McKee, Eye Ubiquitous p15; Hunterian Art Gallery, University of Glasgow, Mackintosh Collection: p10; M.C.Escher's *Metamorphosis 11* c.2000 Cordon Art B.V.-Baarn-Holland. All rights reserved: p22; Oxford Scientific Films: pp6, 8; Photodisc: top and bottom right p7; SCALA: p28; Trevor Clifford: p23; V & A Picture Library: p26; Werner Forman Archive: pp4, 17; Woburn Abbey: p14.

Cover photograph reproduced with permission of Bridgeman Art Library: Arts Council Collection, Hayward Gallery, London.

Every effort has been made to contact copyright holders of any material reproduced in this book. Any omissions will be rectified in subsequent printings if notice is given to the Publisher.

Contents

Any words appearing in the text in bold, **like this**, are explained in the Glossary.

What is a pattern?

Mosaic, Alcazar of Seville, 14th century

A pattern is a shape or **design** which is **repeated**. If you draw a simple shape, colour it and repeat it, you start to build a pattern. Patterns can be simple or complicated. Artists have used pattern for thousands of years, both to **decorate** and to add meaning to their work. Here you can see a **mosaic** from a palace in Spain – not all patterns are as complex as this one though!

Chinatown, New York

In the modern world patterns are everywhere. It is sometimes hard to see them all because there are so many. How many patterns can you find in this picture? The signs, the shapes of the buildings and the vehicles all mix together to make a mass of pattern and colour. You can almost hear the noise! How dull everything would be without pattern.

Patterns and Texture

Nature loves using pattern! We are surrounded by the most complicated and beautiful **designs**. Pattern can change how we see something. Plants can look like stones, insects can look like leaves! Nature makes wonderful patterns everywhere you look. Could you make patterns like these?

stick insect

germander speedwell

butterfly fish

stone flower

garter snake

swallowtail butterfly

tarantula

What do you think the surface of the things on these two pages would be like? Would it be rough or smooth, soft or hard, dry or slippery? The way the surface of an object feels is called its **texture**. Many artists try to show how the things in their pictures would feel if you could really touch them.

Unusual patterns – nature in art

Wind and rain can wear rocks away at different rates. When this happens the effect is sometimes **dramatic**. Sandstone rocks can make particularly colourful patterns in the changing light of day. These patterns have been cut over thousands of years and are still changing today. Do they look as if they are moving? How do you think these rocks would feel?

Rock formation, Colorado, USA

Georgia O'Keeffe, *Out Back of Marie's*, 1930

Have you ever seen hills and mountains look like this?
Georgia O'Keeffe has painted a **landscape** in which the
folds of the rocks seem to be moving. It is as if the land is
alive. The colours, **textures** and patterns the artist has
used can all be found in nature, but she has mixed them
together in her own, very special, way.

Man-made patterns

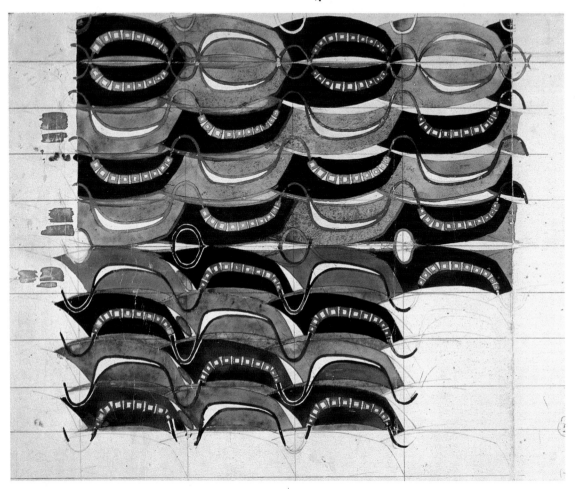

Charles Rennie Mackintosh, *Wave Pattern: Green, Purple, Pink, Orange and Black*, 1915–23

Charles Mackintosh was a Scottish **architect** and designer. He made this **design** to be printed on cloth more than 80 years ago. The patterns move from side to side, and also up and down. Notice how the artist has used a grid to help him make the pattern. Everywhere you look you can see shape, colour and line being **repeated** in this unusual design.

**Chimneys,
Hampton Court
Palace, London,
about 1520**

Patterns and **textures** can be found in the most unlikely of
places! This group of chimneys is at Hampton Court Palace,
near London. The palace was built nearly 500 years ago,
when open fires were the only way of heating a building.
The palace has dozens of chimneys and each one is
different! Why don't you design a chimney pattern yourself?

Shapes make patterns

Do you recognize the shape that is **repeated** here? It is the **continent** of Australia painted in bright, exciting colours. In between these shapes are more traditional **Aboriginal designs**, in black and white. The two parts of the pattern are very different from one another, but they do not clash. Can you see how the dotted black and white lines are used to make space in the picture?

Jeffrey Samuels, *This Changing Continent of Australia*, 1984

Pavel Filonov, *Faces*, 1940

Pavel Filonov was a Russian artist who began painting around 100 years ago. In this picture patterns swirl and **collide**, and suddenly faces can be seen. How many can you find? You should see three. The faces slowly appear from under the patterns and the eyes look straight at you. They seem trapped beneath the ever moving shapes.

Patterns with meaning

Pattern can help make the meaning of a painting clear. Here is a **portrait** of Queen Elizabeth I, painted after England defeated the **Spanish Armada** in 1588. The picture is full of symbols of her power: the crown, her hand on the globe and the Armada sailing to destruction. But look also at her clothes! The fine pattern and **texture** of her dress tell us that this is a very powerful person who can afford expensive clothes, and an artist to paint her!

Artist unknown, *Elizabeth I Armada Portrait*, 1588

Aboriginal man with painted face

People have **decorated** their bodies for thousands of years. Often they do this to make themselves feel special in some way. This **Aboriginal** man has painted his face with stripes and dots. Perhaps he is about to take part in a ceremony. Have you ever had to get dressed up to do something special? How did you feel?

Patterns and texture in nature

Gustav Klimt,
Birch Forest,
1903

Artists often try to copy the patterns they find in nature.
Here the Austrian artist Gustav Klimt has painted a birch
wood in autumn. He has looked very hard at the patterns,
texture and colour of the bark, and has copied the huge
range he has seen. These patterns, textures and colours
make us realize just how special some ordinary places
can be, if we look hard enough.

16

Not all patterns that artists find in nature are complicated. Sometimes the simple ones work just as well. These flowers were painted on a screen in Japan, over 300 years ago. The **delicate** colours and shapes have been perfectly copied by the artist. The leaves, flowers and stems are carefully arranged across the picture space. Does this picture make you feel calm and peaceful?

Japanese painted screen, 17th–18th century

Pattern at work

Barbara Hepworth made this picture shortly after the end of World War II (1939–45). She had spent some time in a hospital and admired the work the **surgeons** did there. The five figures stand in a row, all looking the same way, perhaps at the patient. Three of the surgeons make a **repeated** pattern. Only the position of the hands changes slightly in each person.

Barbara Hepworth, *The Hands*, 1948

Fernand Léger, *Constructors: The Team at Rest, 1950*

The French artist Fernand Léger painted this picture of men putting up a metal frame for a new building. The strong patterns and colours of the building frame support the men at work and those resting. The men's hands are larger than usual because the painting is about **physical** work. The simple, repeated patterns in the building frame and the men's clothes give the picture a tough feel.

**Yvaral
Vasarely,
Untitled,
1965**

In the 1960s, some artists became interested in the special
effects that pattern and light can have on the eye. This
sort of art is called **Op Art**, short for Optical Art. Line and
shape **combine** to make this dazzling pattern. The pattern
is the whole point of the painting, there is nothing else.
Look at this for a while and the shapes can seem to
move. How does this picture make you feel?

20

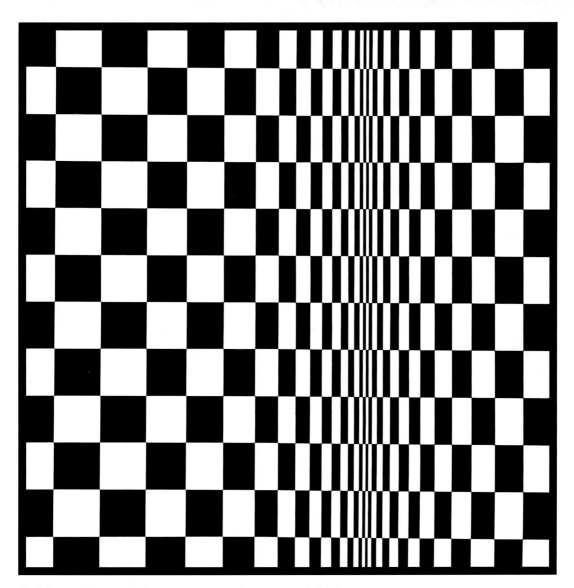

Bridget Riley, *Movement in Squares,* 1962

Another artist who became interested in Op Art was the British painter Bridget Riley. She used just shape and line with no colour, completing a number of pictures in black and white. Some are very difficult to look at for long, because they disturb the eyes so much. It can be difficult to realize that this picture is just a flat surface!

Patterns that fit together

M. C. Escher,
Metamorphosis II,
about 1940

Shapes which fit together with no spaces between them are said to **tessellate**. M. C. Escher, a Dutch artist, made many pictures with shapes that work together to make patterns. How many different patterns and shapes can you see in this very long picture? Look how they change into each other.

A jigsaw piece is a kind of tessellation and is really easy to draw. Copy the jigsaw pieces here, or make up your own. Inside the pieces draw patterns or a picture you like. You could even stick the whole thing onto card and then cut it out to make a real jigsaw.

Pattern, colour and Shape

The Russian artist Kasimir Malevich painted this picture. He used simple shapes and only a few colours. We can see four faceless figures standing in line. Malevich wants to remind us of Russian religious paintings, which often show saints in a line across the picture. The half-white faces and patterned bodies make us wonder what the picture is about.

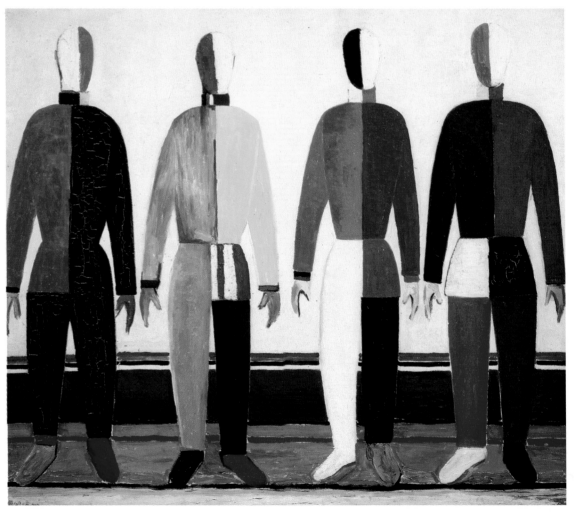

Kasimir Malevich, *The Athletes*, 1928–32

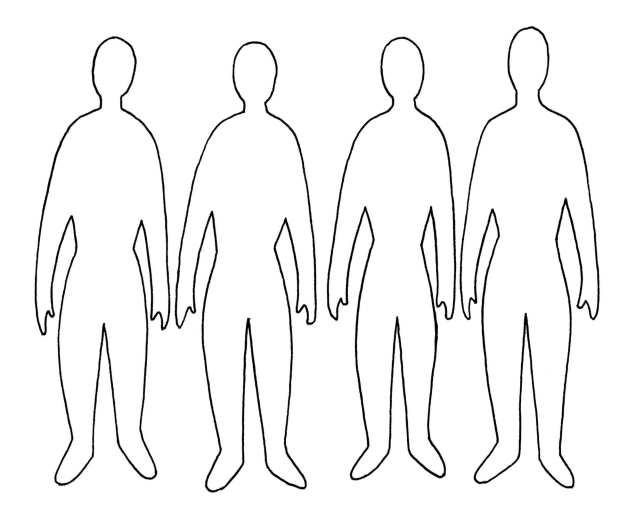

Here is the same picture but without the colours. Copy the four figures onto a large piece of paper, and then colour them with patterns of your own. Don't use too many colours, and keep the patterns simple. Colour part of the background as well. Have you found that, like Malevich, you can put feeling into ordinary shapes using careful colouring?

Making pattern work for you

William Morris was an English artist who designed carpets, furniture, tiles and **stained glass**. In this stained glass **design**, the woman is playing a musical instrument, probably a lute. Morris has **divided** the space around her to look like tiles. The **repeated** patterns of daisies and sunflowers **decorate** the background in a quietly graceful way.

William Morris,
Woman Playing a Lute,
about 1872–74

This is a page from a hand-painted book made more than 1300 years ago. It is much simpler than it looks. Look carefully at the middle four squares (a detail is shown on the right). Can you see how the pattern fits together? Draw some squares and try making your own designs. Keep these simple at first, and make sure the corners match. Try putting a flower or plant in the centre.

Page from the Lindisfarne Gospels, about AD 698

Patterns old and new

Some of the oldest surviving patterns were made by the ancient Egyptians. This is the **sarcophagus** of the pharaoh Tutankhamun, made more than 3000 years ago. Red and blue glass has been **delicately** placed between lines of gold, to create a beautiful pattern. The Egyptians loved bright colours, and often surrounded their art with patterned frames.

Sarcophagus of Tutankhamun, Egypt, about 1323 BC

The next time you paint or draw a picture, put a patterned frame around it. Copy some of the squares below, or **design** your own. Use two or three different squares and **repeat** them to make a frame around your page. If you use only a few colours, perhaps two for each square, you will soon have a **decoration** just as good as the ancient Egyptians made!

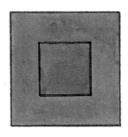

Glossary

Aboriginal native person of Australia

architect person who designs buildings

collide to crash or bump into something

combine to mix together

continent large area of land – Australia, Africa, Europe, North America, South America, Asia and the Antarctic are all continents

decorate to make something more pleasant or interesting to look at

delicate very fine, gentle

design lines and shapes which decorate a picture

divide to split into two or more parts

dramatic something which is surprising or exciting

landscape picture of natural and man-made scenery, for example fields, trees and houses

mosaic picture or pattern made with small coloured stones, glass or tiles

Op Art short for Optical Art. A kind of painting in which lines and colour make the eyes see something which is not real. For example, pictures appear to move.

portrait painting which shows what someone looks like

physical to do with the body

repeat to do something over and over again

sarcophagus coffin

Spanish Armada fleet of ships which sailed from Spain to invade England in 1588

stained glass pieces of coloured glass put together to make a picture

style the way in which a picture is painted

surgeon doctor who performs operations in a hospital

tessellate shapes which fit together with no spaces between them

texture the feel or look of something

Index